Because I Said So!

by Pat Brady

TOPPER BOOKS
AN IMPRINT OF PHAROS BOOKS
A SCRIPPS HOWARD COMPANY
NEW YORK

Copyright © 1989 United Feature Syndicate, Inc.
All rights reserved. No part of this book may be
reproduced in any form or by any means
without permission of the publisher.

ROSE IS ROSE strips © 1986, 1987
United Feature Syndicate, Inc.

Library of Congress Catalog Card Number: 88-043587
Pharos ISBN: 0-88687-434-3

Printed in the United States of America

Topper Books
An Imprint of Pharos Books
A Scripps Howard Company
200 Park Avenue
New York, NY 10166

10 9 8 7 6 5 4 3 2 1

When we were kids

it was such an empty, draining, hopeless feeling

when the book had no pictures.

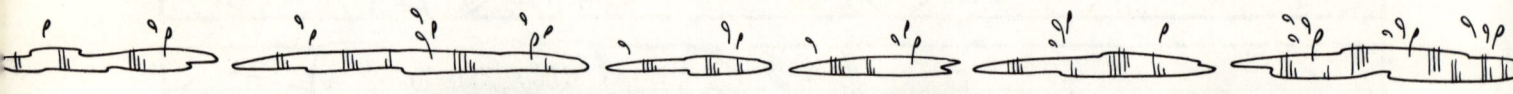

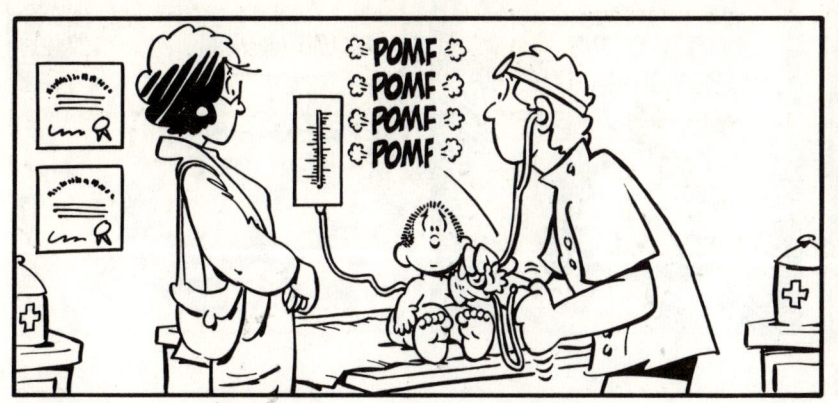

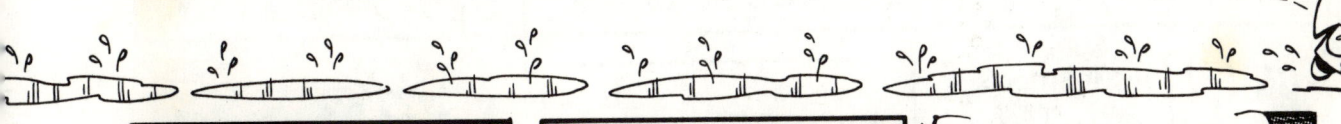

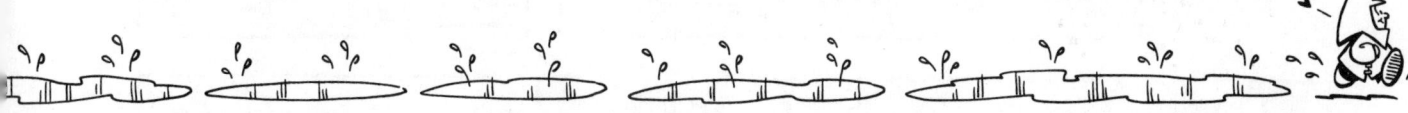

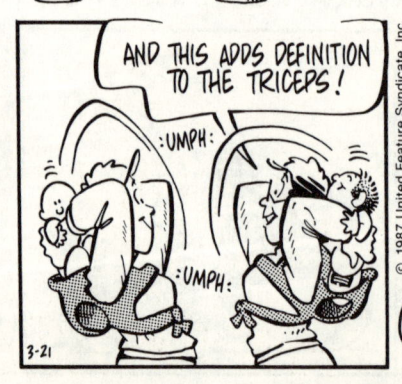

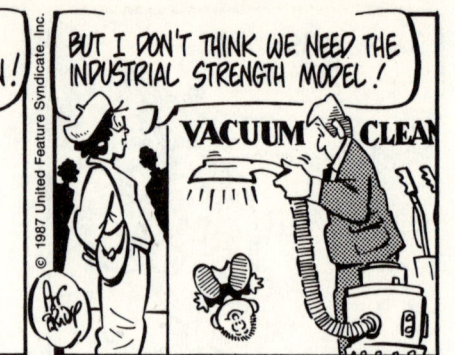